· FI

FISHING DOGS

·

A GUIDE TO THE
HISTORY, TALENTS, AND TRAINING
OF THE BAILDALE, THE FLOUNDERHOUNDER,
THE ANGLER DOG, AND SUNDRY OTHER
BREEDS OF AQUATIC DOGS
(*CANIS PISCATORIUS*)

·

Raymond Coppinger

Illustrated by Peter Pinardi

Secker & Warburg
London

First published in Great Britain in 1997
by Martin Secker & Warburg Limited
an imprint of Reed International Books Limited
Michelin House, 81 Fulham Road, London SW3 6RB
and Auckland, Melbourne, Singapore and Toronto
www.secker.com

A CIP catalogue record for this book
is available from the British Library

ISBN 0 436 20423 1

Typeset in $10\frac{1}{2}$ pt Garamond
by Deltatype Ltd. Birkenhead, Merseyside
Text design by Victor Ichioka
Printed and bound in Great Britain
by Clays Ltd, St Ives plc

· DEDICATION ·

*Since I can't think of anyone better,
I dedicate this book to Stan Warner.*